The Sleepy Seed Fairy

May 14, 2004

Rosalie Snow Albert

Be happy reading!
Love + prayers,
Rosalie Snow Albert

KALLISTI PUBLISHING
WILKES-BARRE, PA

Cover design by Katelyn Kaminski

FIRST EDITION

Published by Kallisti Publishing
332 Center Street, Wilkes-Barre, PA 18702

ISBN: 0-9678514-6-7

The Sleepy Seed Fairy is dedicated to

My grand-daughter,
Danielle Marie Albert

Love and prayers,
Grandmother

Once upon a time in the land of Benton, there lived a beautiful little princess.

Her name was Princess Danielle.

Rosalie Snow Albert

She lived in a big, brick castle with her father, King Dan; her mother, Queen Tina; and her brother, Prince Patrick.

The Sleepy Seed Fairy

Every morning, Princess Danielle would awaken with a big smile on her face.

She was very helpful around the castle and enjoyed playing with the animals.

Rosalie Snow Albert

Princess Danielle was very kind to everyone, but there was one little problem in the life of this beautiful little princess:

She could not fall asleep at night.

4

The Sleepy Seed Fairy

Princess Danielle began worrying about this problem. She began talking to everyone about it. People gave her all different kinds of advice about this problem.

Some people said, "Drink warm milk before bed."

Other people said, "Practice standing on your head for ten minutes before you go to bed."

Everyone had a different solution to the problem.

Finally, her brother, Prince Patrick, told her that she should call on the Sleepy Seed Fairy.

That night when Princess Danielle went to bed, she laid for a long time with her big, blue eyes wide open. She remembered what her big brother, Prince Patrick, had said. Even if the castle had a phone, how and where could she call the Sleepy Seed Fairy?

Princess Danielle drifted off to dream land. In her dreams, the Sleepy Seed Fairy appeared.

The Sleepy Seed Fairy

Princess Danielle sat up in bed. The Sleepy Seed Fairy was standing beside her bed! She spoke to Princess Danielle saying, "Princess Danielle, why have you been calling for me?"

Princess Danielle began to cry. She never cried, so this was very unusual for her. She cried out, "Sleepy Seed Fairy, every night when I go to bed I cannot fall asleep. I am the only one I know who cannot fall asleep. What is wrong with me?"

The Sleepy Seed Fairy smiled. She replied, "My dear little Princess Danielle, I will do whatever I can to help you. What do you want me to do?"

Princess Danielle answered with a sigh, "At night I cannot fall asleep, but in the morning when I awake, I have sleepy seeds in my eyes. If you would help me find some sleepy seeds, I could put them in my eyes at night. I think the sleepy seeds would help me fall asleep."

The Sleepy Seeds Fairy nodded her head. She spoke very softly, "I'm not sure where you can find sleepy seeds. If you feel you must look for them, I will give you a list of places to look."

7

The next morning, Princess Danielle went very quickly down the long staircase to join the royal family for breakfast. Her mind was not on breakfast, but instead it was on the long list of places the Sleepy Seed Fairy had given her to look for sleepy seeds.

Her mother, Queen Tina, called for the royal carriage and she and Princess Danielle left the castle on their journey to search for—and hopefully find—the miracle sleepy seeds.

The royal carriage took Queen Tina and Princess Danielle to the local toy store. There the little princess asked for help locating sleepy seeds. She was sent to different departments of the toy store where clerks shook their heads and said, "No, we don't carry sleepy seeds in this department."

The royal carriage moved on to the local grocery store. Again, the clerks shook their heads and said, "No, not here."

The royal carriage went from place to place, store to store. The answer was always the same: "No, not here."

Finally, the royal carriage arrived at the last place on the list: the local drug store. Princess Danielle hurried inside. She was certain that the miracle sleepy seeds would be found here.

The local pharmacists shook his head. He suggested, "Princess Danielle, have you thought about saving your own sleepy seeds to be used the next night?"

Princess Danielle thanked the pharmacist because she was very polite. Immediately, the royal carriage was directed to return to the castle.

That night, Princess Danielle could hardly await for bedtime to arrive. She very quickly said her prayers and closed her eyes in sleep.

The next morning, she took her sleepy seeds from her eyes and placed them very carefully on her night stand.

She would never have to worry about going to sleep again!

The Sleepy Seed Fairy

Night arrived and Princess Danielle ran up to her castle bedroom. Oh! Oh! Where were her sleepy seeds? Hadn't she been polite when she instructed the maid to be very careful with the miracle sleepy seeds?

Princess Danielle knew that sleepy seeds only appear after a night's sleep. So after asking a lot of questions and looking everywhere, she closed her eyes and went to sleep. When morning arrived, Princess Danielle cautiously placed the new magic sleepy seeds in a clear bottle with a very tight cover. She happily hurried down the long staircase to begin a new day.

What a surprise it was that night when Princess Danielle opened the bottle and looked inside. There were no sleepy seeds inside the bottle! They had disappeared once again. She could not worry about sleepy seeds tonight. She had a soccer game scheduled for tomorrow and wanted to get some sleep.

Princess Danielle had just closed her eyes when the Sleepy Seed Fairy appeared to her again.

"Princess Danielle," she said patiently, "I have tried in many ways to help you. Sleepy seeds are only used one time. They disappear after they have been used. I thought when I sent you to several stores and you discovered they were not for sale, you would understand that they are a very special part of you. But then, when you tried to save them, I knew that you did not understand the magic of your body and the life within it. I will ask you to let me go. You no longer need a Sleepy Seed Fairy. You now know that when you want to go to sleep, you can. Magic sleepy seeds are not necessary."

Princess Danielle smiled a big smile. What a relief to have this over! Tomorrow, she would feed the animals, play soccer, and go on with her life. She was very grateful to the Sleepy Seed Fairy, but now she needed to get back to sleep.

15